From Meltdowns to Coping Skills

Parenting with ADHD

Table of Contents

Chapter 1. Introduction

Welcome to our eye-opening Special Report, "From Meltdowns to Coping Skills: Parenting with ADHD." Are you a parent searching for understanding, comfort, and effective strategies to navigate the tumultuous waters of ADHD with your child? Or perhaps you're a caregiver looking to help your loved ones deal with situations that may not always be within their control? Whatever your relationship to this topic, this comprehensive guide promises a journey towards greater understanding and confidence. Combining expert insights, first-hand narratives, practical advice, and heartwarming success stories, this report is an invaluable tool kit destined to bring light into your everyday parenting or caregiving experiences. Trust us; by the time you've reached the end, you'll wonder how you ever managed without it.

Chapter 2. Understanding ADHD: Grounding Facts and Dispelling Myths

Attention-Deficit/Hyperactivity Disorder (ADHD) is a developmental disorder, more prevalent in children and often extends into adolescence and adulthood. Its prominent features include difficulty in sustaining attention, hyperactivity, and impulsivity. Let us embark on a detailed journey to understand this complex disorder, grounding it in facts and dispelling its frequent myths.

2.1. Grounding Facts

ADHD is not a "one-size-fits-all" disorder; it manifests in different forms and degrees, morphing different identities in different individuals. Here are some facts that will establish a firm foundation in understanding ADHD:

1. **Prevalence:** According to the American Psychiatric Association, about 5% of children have ADHD. However, studies in the community show higher numbers. The CDC states that approximately 11% of American children, aged between 4 and 17 years, have been diagnosed with ADHD at some point in their lives.

2. **Types of ADHD:** ADHD is of three types, Predominantly Inattentive Presentation, Predominantly Hyperactive-Impulsive Presentation, and Combined Presentation. The symptoms of inattention and/or hyperactivity and impulsivity have been present for six months or more to a degree that is disruptive and inappropriate for the individual's developmental level in these types.

3. **Diagnosis**: Diagnosis of ADHD requires a comprehensive

evaluation by a licensed clinician, such as a pediatrician, psychologist, or psychiatrist with expertise in ADHD. For a person to receive a diagnosis of ADHD, the symptoms should be chronic or long-lasting, impair the person's functioning, and cause the person to fall behind typical development for his or her age.

4. **Cause**: The exact cause of ADHD is unknown, but it has a strong genetic component. Other factors contributing might include low birth weight, smoking, alcohol and drug use during pregnancy.

5. **Treatment**: ADHD is usually treated using a combination of behavioral therapy, counseling, and medications. Although it cannot be "cured," these treatments can help manage symptoms effectively.

Now that we have established the fundamental facts about ADHD, it is high time to dispel some myths accompanying this disorder.

2.2. Dispelling Myths

While ADHD has gained considerable attention over the years, several misconceptions persist. Here we address and dismiss these myths so that misunderstandings don't cloud our perceptions:

1. **Myth: "ADHD isn't a real medical disorder."**

ADHD is recognized as a legitimate diagnosis by major medical, psychological, and educational organizations, including the National Institutes of Health and the U.S. Department of Education. The American Psychiatric Association recognizes ADHD as a medical disorder in its Diagnostic and Statistical Manual of Mental Disorders ▯ the official mental health manual used by psychologists and psychiatrists.

2. **Myth: "All kids with ADHD are hyperactive."**

Not all children who have ADHD are hyperactive. Some children may exhibit signs of hyperactivity and impulsivity, but others may just have the inattentive type of ADHD. These students may be overlooked because they're not disrupting the class or misbehaving.

3. **Myth: "Only boys have ADHD."**

While ADHD is more commonly diagnosed in boys, it is also diagnosed in girls. Because girls often exhibit less overt symptoms than boys, such as inattentiveness and less hyperactivity, they may be overlooked.

4. **Myth: "ADHD is caused by bad parenting."**

No evidence suggests that ADHD is the result of neglectful or lax parenting. The main factors contributing to ADHD are largely genetic and neurological, not environmental. While the environment can exacerbate symptoms, it does not cause the disorder.

5. **Myth: "Children with ADHD eventually outgrow their condition."**

While some children find their symptoms decrease with age, many continue to struggle into adolescence and adulthood. It's a lifelong condition that needs

As we unveil the realities and dismiss myths associated with ADHD, we better position ourselves to understand, support, and guide children in their unique journey. Remember that while ADHD poses challenges, it doesn't define the person. Each child is unique, with their unique strengths and difficulties. Recognizing this uniqueness is a crucial step towards creating a supportive environment that embraces all children.

Chapter 3. The ADHD Brain: An Inside Look

Our journey begins with understanding the brain affected by Attention-Deficit/Hyperactivity Disorder (ADHD). Becoming familiar with this integral body organ and the effects of ADHD on its functions forms the foundation of our approach to parenting or caregiving for individuals with ADHD.

3.1. Understanding ADHD

ADHD is a neurodevelopmental disorder often diagnosed during childhood, although it's not uncommon for a person to receive a diagnosis during adulthood. ADHD characteristically presents with symptoms such as difficulty paying attention, hyperactivity, and impulsive behavior. These symptoms often interfere with the person's daily life, influencing their academic progress, job performance, and interpersonal relationships.

3.2. The Typical Brain Vs. The ADHD Brain

The brain, the center of our nervous system, is composed of billions of nerve cells that communicate with each other via neurotransmitters, forming a network of intricate connections. In a brain unaffected by ADHD, information flows smoothly from one nerve cell to another, resulting in a balance between different brain activities.

But the brain's landscape is notably different in a person with ADHD. Research indicates that certain areas of the brain may be smaller, particularly regions responsible for attentiveness and impulse control. Also, neurochemical processes involved in communicating information may be disrupted, leading to challenges in sustaining attention, controlling impulse, and managing behavior.

3.3. Understanding Neurotransmitters

Neurotransmitters are chemicals that carry signals across the brain. Two key neurotransmitters, dopamine and norepinephrine, play crucial roles in the ADHD brain.

Dopamine is involved in our brain's reward system and plays a role in pleasure, motivation, and learning. In individuals with ADHD, dopamine levels may be lower than average or dopamine pathways may be functioning sub-optimally. This could potentially explain why people with ADHD often seek immediate rewards or have difficulty staying motivated for tasks that don't offer instant gratification.

Norepinephrine regulates attention and arousal. It assists in focusing attention on tasks and may have a role in impulse control. A deficiency, or imbalanced distribution of norepinephrine, can contribute to the traits of inattentiveness and impulsivity common in ADHD.

It's important to note that the relationships between neurotransmitters and ADHD symptoms are complex and not yet fully understood. While these neurotransmitter systems are often the focus of medicinal treatment strategies, they represent just one component of the bigger picture.

3.4. Brain Regions and ADHD

There are several key brain regions that are affected in ADHD, each playing a different role in the behaviors observed.

The prefrontal cortex, located in the front of the brain, is responsible for executive functions. It's like the brain's control panel, regulating attention, impulse control, organization skills, and decision-making. In the ADHD brain, this region may be smaller and show less activity, possibly contributing to difficulties in executive functioning.

The basal ganglia, a group of structures in the center of the brain, coordinates messages between multiple brain regions. In individuals with ADHD, the basal ganglia may be smaller or have decreased activity, potentially disrupting the transmission of nerve signals involved in attention and behavior management.

The anterior cingulate cortex regulates emotional control. This brain region helps one respond appropriately to emotionally significant events and suppress impulses that could lead to inappropriate reactions. Again, changes in the size or function of this region could potentially contribute to the emotional dysregulation often seen in ADHD.

3.5. Epigenetics and ADHD

Another aspect of ADHD involves epigenetics, which is the study of changes in organism's gene expression that don't involve alterations to the underlying DNA sequence. It's like looking at how environmental factors can turn our genes "on" or "off." In terms of ADHD, certain gene expressions may be influenced by environmental triggers, which could contribute to the disorder's manifestation and explains why ADHD can sometimes run in families.

3.6. The Impact of ADHD on the Brain

ADHD affects the brain's structure, function, and chemistry, leading to the observed behavioral symptoms. However, understanding these changes can guide effective management strategies. Therapies used in treatment aim to improve the specific areas of dysfunction in the brain, leading to improvements in attention, self-control, and other impacted areas.

The ADHD brain may present unique challenges, but it also offers the potential for unique strengths. Its novelty-seeking nature can fuel creativity, and its quick rates of information processing can enhance problem-solving skills in certain situations.

Our exploration of the ADHD brain offers a springboard to better understand, empathize, and support individuals with ADHD. It is the first step in transforming perceived obstacles into stepping stones towards success for the ones you care for. Let this insight serve as a guiding lamp on your path towards more successful ADHD parenting or caregiving.

Chapter 4. Impact of ADHD on Daily Life: A Molecular Perspective

Attention-Deficit/Hyperactivity Disorder (ADHD) can greatly affect everyday life. However, examining its impact from a molecular perspective can provide fascinating insights, and more importantly, offer potential solutions that could ease the struggles those with ADHD experience.

4.1. The Molecular Basis of ADHD

It's clear from numerous studies over the years that ADHD does have a genetic component. While no single gene or gene variant has emerged as "the ADHD gene," several have been found in correlation with the disorder. These include DRD4, a dopamine receptor gene; DAT1, which helps control the uptake of dopamine into neurons; and ADRA2A, an adrenaline receptor gene. This genetic aspect implies that there are molecular mechanisms at play in ADHD, influencing how individuals experience and respond to the world.

Dopamine and norepinephrine are two neurotransmitters that are often mentioned concerning ADHD. They play critical roles in attention, motivation, and reward systems in the brain. In the current understanding, ADHD is often associated with diminished quantities or irregular function of these neurotransmitters in certain brain areas. Individuals with ADHD typically have less efficient and less predictable release patterns of these critical neurotransmitters.

Recent research has pin-pointed variations in dopamine and serotonin transporter genes, which are involved in clearing these neurotransmitters from the synapse, the small gap between neurons. Differences in these transporter genes can increase the speed at which these neurotransmitters are cleared away. Faster clearance means less time for neurotransmitters to do their work – contributing to problems with focusing and impulsivity. Conversely, slower-than-average clearance contributes to prolonged periods of arousal, leading to hyperactivity.

4.2. Neurological Impact of ADHD

Examining ADHD from a neurological perspective gives us an insight into the molecular imbalances behind ADHD behavior. For instance, the prefrontal cortex of the brain, responsible for executive functioning tasks like decision-making, impulse control, attention, and emotional regulation, seems to function differently among those with ADHD.

The neurochemical interplay within the prefrontal cortex typically enables individuals to sustain attention, resist distraction, and regulate their impulsive responses. However, with ADHD, the sufficient availability of dopamine and norepinephrine is often compromised, disrupting the normal functioning of this area. As a result, the tasks managed by this region can become formidable challenges for those with ADHD.

4.3. ADHD and Daily Life

Given the molecular and neurological aspects of ADHD, its impact on daily life can be wide-ranging. Since the brain regulates so much of our behavior, changes in brain chemistry can manifest as struggles with organization, focus, impulsivity, emotional regulation, and hyperactivity. These might affect a person's academic performance, career progression, relationships, and overall quality of life.

For individuals with ADHD, simple daily tasks like staying organized, keeping appointments, and maintaining a structured routine can be challenging. They may find it difficult to juggle multiple responsibilities simultaneously or follow directions consistently.

Impulsivity, another common characteristic, might manifest in many ways - from impulsive spending, decision-making without considering long-term consequences, to interrupting others in conversation. These behavioral patterns can create friction in relationships and professional settings.

Hyperactivity and restlessness, especially in children with ADHD, can lead to excessive physical activity, feelings of restlessness, and difficulty engaging in quiet or restful activities. These symptoms can interfere with academic settings requiring extended periods of focus and calm.

4.4. Coping Strategies and the Promise of Modern Medicine

Having explored the molecular underpinnings of ADHD and seen its impact on daily life, it's encouraging to find that a molecular understanding also paves the way for viable solutions. Medications, such as stimulant and non-stimulant drugs, have been shown to increase the availability of dopamine and norepinephrine in the brain, improving symptoms for many individuals with ADHD.

Medications, however, aren't the only answer. Behavior therapy, cognitive behavioral therapy, and mindfulness-based therapies have all seen success in managing ADHD symptoms, teaching individuals to better control their focus, impulses, and hyperactivity, providing a reprieve from their molecular challenges.

It's clear that a molecular understanding of ADHD can drastically enhance our approach to managing this disorder. By comprehending the ways in which brain chemistry affects behavior, potential treatments can be tailored to specific molecular mechanisms, leading to improved daily living and overall quality-of-life for those living with ADHD. This opens possibilities for personalized treatments that operate on an individual's unique genetic makeup - marking a promising future for those affected by ADHD. Although understanding ADHD from a molecular perspective may be complex, it certainly provides a breadth of opportunities to alleviate the persistent challenges that come with the condition.

In conclusion, it takes tremendous strength to parent or care for a child with ADHD, and armed with this understanding, the journey can become somewhat less turbulent. Knowledge is power, and an understanding of the molecular facets of ADHD can be a potent tool in managing the daily challenges that come with this disorder.

Chapter 5. Beyond the Meltdown: Unraveling the Meaning

Understanding meltdowns lie at the heart of parenting a child with ADHD. Meltdowns are not just a sign of a child trying to get their own way—they represent a fundamental part of ADHD, one that can be hard for parents and caregivers to comprehend.

5.1. The Anatomy of a Meltdown

Meltdowns are periods of intense emotional distress, where the child feels a loss of control over their emotions and sensations. They are not intentional displays of disobedience or disrespect, but reactions to stimuli or situations that overwhelm their processing abilities.

Children with ADHD often experience 'sensory overload' - where multiple sensory inputs cause intense discomfort and stress. This could be due to loud noises, tactile discomfort, strong smells, or bright lights. Situations that demand a lot of concentration can also trigger a meltdown.

Understanding what causes these meltdowns is the first step towards formulating an effective coping strategy.

5.2. Unearthing the Emotions

To better understand the challenging behavior, it's essential to go beyond the surface and dig deeper into the wells of emotion bubbled beneath. ADHD children often face difficulty articulating their feelings, making it harder for us to comprehend the depth of their emotional undercurrents.

ADHD is characterized by impulsivity, inattention, and hyperactivity, but emotional dysregulation is another critical component. Sensitized emotional responses, intense reactions to minor provocations, and rapid mood swings are all common characteristics.

These emotional responses are not manufactured; they are genuine. It's as if the dial on their emotion meter is turned up higher than for most people. Recognizing and acknowledging these intense feelings is crucial to helping your child move beyond the meltdown.

5.3. Amplified Reactions: More than Being 'Dramatic'

To an outsider, an ADHD child's emotional responses can seem excessive. The phrase "making a mountain out of a molehill" often comes into play. However, within the child's experience, the onslaught of emotions can feel like an unconquerable mountain.

This is because those with ADHD often have an intensified experience of emotion. That's not the same as overreacting or being dramatic: it's a real, physiological response that's not within their conscious control. This 'emotional impulsivity' can make it difficult to employ rational thought, worsen feelings of distress, and exacerbate the intensity of their meltdown.

5.4. Stress And Overwhelm: The Causal Factors

Stress can be a significant component of ADHD, stemming from a variety of sources. These can include academic struggles, social difficulties, and the constant pressure to conform to social norms.

Many children with ADHD also have trouble with executive functions. These are the brain-based skills required for dealing with tasks, such as planning, focusing attention, remembering instructions, and juggling multiple tasks. Any task requiring executive functions can trigger stress and, potentially, a meltdown.

Overwhelm can occur when the demands on the child's self-control exceed their capacity to deal with them. It's like an elastic band being stretched to its limit; at some point, it will snap. The snap, in this case, is a meltdown.

The overload isn't always external. It can be an internal sensory overload or a combination of both. When we recognize these causative factors, we take a significant step toward addressing and preventing meltdown instances.

5.5. Navigating The Aftermath

The post-meltdown period can be confusing and overwhelming for both the child and the parent. The child often feels regret, shame, or embarrassment about the meltdown, and a parent might feel a range of emotions from frustration to helplessness.

It is essential, at such times, to keep communication channels open, demonstrating love and reassurance. Instead of reprimands, focus on comfort and understanding. Remember, a calm and non-judgmental approach is your most potent tool in the aftermath of a meltdown.

From this understanding stems the chance to develop effective coping mechanisms and strategies that reduce the frequency and intensity of meltdowns. And when they do occur, you'll be armed with the understanding to support your child through it and help them regain their equilibrium.

Take some time. The journey from meltdowns to mastering coping skills isn't always linear or swift. But with patience, understanding, empathy, and the right strategies, you'll definitely see progress.

Chapter 6. Navigating Academics: Excelling with ADHD

Teetering on the intricate balance of academic expectations and the unique challenges imposed by ADHD, many parents and caregivers would undoubtedly attest that their most trying moments often revolve around education. Let's embark on this deep dive into how we can successfully navigate the world of academics with ADHD.

6.1. Understanding ADHD in the Academic Environment

ADHD's manifestations are diverse, often impacting attention, organization, time management, and emotional regulation. These traits inevitably interfere with a child's academic performance, but it's crucial to remember that your child's struggles aren't an indication of their intellectual abilities or potential success.

Understanding how an ADHD brain functions is the first step toward effective coping strategies. Compared to their peers, children with ADHD might have difficulty maintaining concentration, following instructions, or staying organized. They may often lose their belongings and have a harder time handling long-term projects or homework.

6.2. Employing Structured Learning Techniques

Consistency, repetition, and structure aid immensely in managing ADHD symptoms. Structuring the academic environment becomes a vital strategy for aiding your child's educational journey.

Simplify tasks: Break down projects into manageable pieces, employing to-do lists and step-by-step instructions. This technique can lessen the overwhelm accompanying extensive tasks.

Use visual aids: Flowcharts, diagrams, and graphic organizers can assist in understanding and retaining information. Make good use of the technology available; apps such as Mindomo or Google Drawings can be effective tools.

6.3. Building an Adaptive Learning Space

An optimal learning environment for a child with ADHD is one that minimizes distractions and encourages focus.

Design a dedicated study area: Keep this space clutter-free, quiet, and well-lit. Consider investing in noise-cancelling headphones or white noise machines if your child is easily distracted by sounds.

Material organization: School materials should have designated spaces. Labeling and having a system for storing books, notebooks, and school supplies can prevent misplacements and promote organization.

6.4. Encouraging Active Learning

For a child with ADHD, engaging in active learning can be particularly beneficial.

Physical Activity: Just a few minutes of physical activity can boost concentration. Short exercise intervals or walks can be beneficial between study sessions.

Hands-on Learning: Whenever possible, incorporate hands-on activities into learning. Children with ADHD often find experiential learning easier to engage with and remember.

6.5. Fostering Time Management Skills

Time is an abstract concept, and children with ADHD often struggle with managing it effectively.

Use clocks and timers: Visual cues help children understand the concept of time. Use countdown timers during study sessions to give a sense of time left.

Break down time: Split larger durations into smaller, manageable segments, which can prevent overwhelm and provide a sense of achievement as each segment is completed.

6.6. Developing Study Skills

Studying effectively is a challenge for children with ADHD, but with practice and the right techniques, it can be achieved.

Note-taking: Teach your child how to summarize information in their own words instead of copying verbatim. Techniques such as Cornell method or mind maps can be useful.

Breaks During Study: Allow short breaks during study sessions. A technique like the Pomodoro method could be beneficial, where the child works for a specified period, say 25 minutes, and then has a five-minute break.

6.7. Emotional Support and Encouragement

Complementing these practical strategies, emotional support can't be understated.

Positive Reinforcement: Celebrate successes, no matter how small. Praising effort over results encourages perseverance and cultivates a growth mindset.

Open Conversations: Keep communication channels open. Let your child express their struggles or fears about academics without judgment or immediate advice.

6.8. Collaborating with Educators

Your child doesn't tread this complicated path alone. Teachers can be invaluable allies.

Regular Communication: Stay in regular contact with teachers about your child's performance, and discuss appropriate modifications or accommodations.

IEP and 504 plans: If your child's ADHD significantly affects their academics, consider an Individualized Education Program (IEP) or 504 plan. These provide legal protections and ensure your child receives the necessary support.

Fully appreciating that academic success is a marathon, not a sprint, is vital when it comes to ADHD. Guiding your child or loved one through their educational journey may be winding, replete with unanticipated turns, but with these strategies, you can mitigate challenges, nurture resilience, and usher in victories that extend beyond the classroom. Cultivating not just successful learners but also confident, content individuals becomes a fulfilling possibility within your reach.

Chapter 7. Unlocking the Potential: Strengths and Talents of Kids with ADHD

Attention-Deficit/Hyperactivity Disorder (ADHD) is a complex condition that can present both challenges and opportunities. Underpinning these challenges are a set of unique strengths and talents found in kids with ADHD, often including creativity, hyperfocus, resilience, and empathy. It's our mission to help you channel these qualities, unlocking the potential within your child and helping them thrive.

7.1. Understanding ADHD in Children

ADHD is often misconstrued as a deficit or inherent failing, but it's essential to see it as a different way of thinking and processing the world. It's characterized by persistent patterns of inattention, impulsivity, and sometimes hyperactivity that interferes with functioning or development. Common signs include difficulty paying attention, restlessness, and impulsivity.

However, children with ADHD aren't just bundles of symptoms. They have unique thought processes, heightened emotions, energies, and talents. Seeing ADHD this way — an alternative neurological style — allows us to approach it not as a problem to be solved but as a potential to be nurtured.

7.2. Strengths of Children with ADHD

While the challenges faced by children with ADHD are well-documented, their potential strengths are often overlooked. Here are some inherent qualities that most ADHD kids possess:

1. Creativity: Kids with ADHD are often incredibly creative. Their minds race with ideas, thoughts, and possibilities, leading to a deep well of innovation and inventiveness.

2. Hyperfocus: While attention can be a challenge, when children with ADHD find something that grabs their interest, they can focus intensely, often exceeding their peers.

3. Resilience: The challenges they face can lead ADHD kids to develop resilience and adaptability that will serve them well in life.

4. Empathy: Many children with ADHD are highly sensitive to the emotions of others. This can foster deep connections and empathic abilities.

The key to helping children with ADHD lies not only in managing the symptoms but also in nurturing their strengths.

7.3. Nurtishing Strengths and Talents

The environment children grow up in significantly influences their growth and development. For children with ADHD, the home can be a sanctuary where their skills can be nurtured and celebrated.

1. Value Their Creativity: Encourage creative outlets for your kids — it could be drawing, painting, storytelling, or music. A supportive environment can help a child explore and develop their creative

instincts.

2. Foster Hyperfocus: Spot opportunities that align with their interest and engage them in those activities. This will allow them to use their hyperfocus positively and productively.

3. Develop Resilience: Encourage kids when they face setbacks, helping them see failures as opportunities for learning. Also, remind them of their problem-solving abilities to deal with challenges.

4. Encourage Empathy: Nurture their empathic abilities by encouraging discussions about emotions. Reading books or watching shows that explore feelings can also be useful.

7.4. ADHD and Education: Facilitating Learning

School can pose challenges for kids with ADHD, but with the right tools and techniques, it can also be an environment where they thrive. Here are some strategies:

1. Personalized Learning: Recognize different learning styles. Some ADHD kids learn more effectively through movement or hands-on activities.

2. Break Tasks: Large tasks can feel overwhelming. Break them into smaller, manageable parts to reduce anxiety and foster a sense of accomplishment.

3. Encouragement and Praise: Positive reinforcement boosts self-esteem and motivation. Choose to focus more on what they do right.

4. Collaborate with Teachers: Keep open communication with teachers. Share successes at home and any strategies you've found effective.

7.5. Celebrating Progress and Success

Every child develops at their own pace, and progress can sometimes be slow. It's easy to get caught up in the day-to-day struggles and lose sight of the longer journey. Celebrating every small victory can keep moral high and keep everyone motivated.

This journey isn't just about 'curing' or 'fixing'; it's about understanding and maximizing potential. Every child with ADHD is unique, with their own set of strengths, talents, and abilities. By nurturing these, we can help them create a path towards a successful, contented life.

Our hope is that by unlocking these potentials and providing the right environment, ADHD can be reframed from a deficit to a different perspective of expertise that your child brings into the world. The potential found in children with ADHD is enormous — all it awaits is recognition, understanding, and nurturing.

Chapter 8. Holistic Approaches: A Spotlight on Nutrition and Lifestyle

In our exploration of holistic approaches to managing Attention Deficit Hyperactivity Disorder (ADHD), we shine a light on two critical aspects: nutrition and lifestyle changes. Understanding these areas offers a dual-pronged approach towards alleviating some of the challenges ADHD presents, thereby empowering you as a parent or caregiver to facilitate a healthier and calmer environment for your child or ward.

8.1. A Nutritional Perspective

Reflecting on ADHD from a nutritional viewpoint opens up a new lens of understanding. Diet and nutrition can play pivotal roles in managing the symptoms. While it doesn't suggest a cure, it can indeed help moderate and manage the impact.

Diets for children with ADHD have been a topic of extensive research. The typical advice revolves around maintaining a balanced diet - one rich in proteins, fruits, vegetables, and whole grains. However, it's worth noting that there's no one-size-fits-all approach. Every individual is unique and might respond differently to dietary changes. Detailed below are some nutritional strategies that can potentially help manage ADHD symptoms.

8.1.1. Elimination Diets

Symptom reduction through the elimination of certain food substances has been the subject of many scientific inquiries. Although the results are mixed, some individuals respond positively to these dietary modifications.

A widely-discussed elimination diet is the Feingold diet, initially designed to target learning disabilities. The approach primarily involves removing artificial colorings and preservatives, recommending instead a diet loaded with organic and fresh foods. While it has proven beneficial for some, it's critical to seek professional advice before implementing this strategy.

8.1.2. Food Sensitivity and Allergy Testing

The idea that food sensitivities or allergies contribute to ADHD symptoms is gaining traction. Possible culprits could be dairy products, eggs, chocolate, and even common additives like monosodium glutamate (MSG). Discovering a child's specific sensitivities or allergies can help tailor a diet plan that minimizes adverse food interactions.

8.1.3. Essential Fatty Acids (EFAs)

EFAs, such as omega-3 and omega-6 fatty acids, continue to receive attention for their potential impact on brain function and behavior. While the study results vary, increased intake of EFAs - found predominantly in fish oils and flaxseeds - could improve ADHD symptoms for some individuals.

It's common for individuals with ADHD to overlook the enormous role nutrition plays. But nourishment goes hand in hand with medication and counseling to collectively manage the condition.

8.2. A Lifestyle Upgrade

In addition to implementing nutritional changes, modifying lifestyle aspects could go a long way in helping children cope with ADHD. Let's dive into this untapped pool of potential solutions.

8.2.1. Exercise and ADHD

Physical activity is a natural mood lifter and a fantastic way to channel excess energy. It helps stimulate brain chemicals such as dopamine and norepinephrine, playing a significant role in regulating attention and behavior.

Regular physical activity such as swimming, running, dancing, or even a simple game of catch can provoke positive changes. Organized sports can also be beneficial, not just for physical exertion but also for the development of social skills and self-esteem.

8.2.2. Sleep Routines

Many children and adolescents with ADHD struggle with sleep issues, which can exacerbate attention and behavior problems. Regular sleep routines can help. This could involve setting a consistent bedtime, creating a relaxing sleep environment, limiting screen time before bed, and establishing calming pre-sleep rituals such as reading or bathing.

8.2.3. Mindfulness and Relaxation Techniques

Maintaining a calm, zen-like home environment can help manage ADHD symptoms. Techniques such as yoga, deep breathing exercises, and meditation can be great tools to introduce calm and order amidst the usual tumult.

Neurofeedback, a form of biofeedback that uses real-time displays of brain activity to promote self-regulation of brain function, is another your child might find interesting and helpful.

8.3. Tying the Knot Between Nutrition and Lifestyle

Positively modifying a child's diet and lifestyle together can constitute a powerful tool in your arsenal against the trials of ADHD. By focusing on these elements, parents and caregivers can make a significant difference in the child's day-to-day interactions and overall growth trajectory.

The journey is unique to each individual dealing with ADHD. Catering to this uniqueness and forging a holistic plan with a foundation on nutrition and lifestyle changes is the way forward. Providing a nurturing and understanding environment coupled with these strategies will go a long way in helping your child thrive.

ADHD can be a difficult journey, but remember, it's a marathon, not a sprint. Celebrate small victories, practice patience, and keep going. Through nutrition, lifestyle changes, and a heap of love and understanding, you and your child can traverse this path to a happier, healthier life.

Chapter 9. Practical Strategies: Creating an ADHD-Friendly Home and Routine

One of the most practical steps you can take to assist your child with ADHD is creating an ADHD-friendly environment at home. We're not merely talking about an organized space, but also about implementing a sustainable routine that encourages your child's development. By implementing some of the strategies listed below, you can help your child to navigate their day-to-day life with ease and confidence.

9.1. Structure their surroundings

Children with ADHD typically operate best in an organized setting. This provides them with a sense of control, making it easier to focus and complete tasks. When organizing your home, aim to create designated spaces for specific activities. For instance, establish a quiet, clutter-free area for study, and a different space for play.

1. **Foster a Study-friendly Environment:** Choose a quiet location in your house, preferably away from distractions. No clutter, just the essential study resources at hand. Having a dedicated study area sends a subliminal message to your child that it's time to concentrate and learn. Moreover, having all study-related materials in one place minimizes opportunities for distraction during study hours.

2. **Encourage 'Zone Living':** Implement the principle of 'Zone Living'; this involves identifying different areas in the house for different activities. For example, designate the living room as a

'quiet zone' and the backyard or a playroom as a 'go wild zone'. This helps your child to associate specific behaviors with particular areas of your home, creating more predictability.

9.2. Stick to a routine

Children with ADHD often find it easier to manage their behavior and maintain concentration when their days are structured consistently. Establishing a regular routine will help them to understand what is expected of them and when.

1. **Create a Daily Schedule:** Maintain a consistent schedule that includes wake-up time, school hours, homework time, meals, recreational activities, chores, and bedtimes. This kind of routine offers a feeling of security and helps your child understand what to expect next. Make sure this schedule is visible and refer back to it regularly.

2. **Balance Busy and Downtime:** While keeping a routine is crucial, allowing for flexibility is equally important. Not every minute of your child's day should be scheduled. Ensure there is sufficient downtime for relaxation and free play.

3. **Nighttime Routine:** Establishing a sound nighttime routine can be particularly beneficial. Prepare your child for sleep by regularly practicing calming activities such as reading a book or taking a warm bath before bed. Reducing screen time or any stimulating activities close to sleep is also important.

9.3. Encourage physical activity

Physical activity can be a wonderful outlet for kids with ADHD. It not only helps in burning off excess energy but also improves concentration and promotes better sleep.

1. **Include Physical Activity in the Daily Routine:** Make sure you

include some form of exercise in your child's daily routine. Whether it's a sport, dancing, yoga or even simple activities like jumping rope or playing catch, what's important is that they're moving their body.

2. **Family Workout Time:** Engage the whole family in physical activity. This not only sets a good example but also makes exercise more fun.

9.4. Support their studies

While school provides the bulk of educational time, your home can also help support your child's learning process. From creating a conducive learning area to actively participating in their schoolwork, there's a lot you can do to assist.

1. **Stay Connected with Teachers:** Regular communication with your child's teachers can provide insights into your child's progress and challenges. You can also explore supplemental resources and study techniques based on their recommendations.

2. **Homework Diary:** Teach your child to maintain a homework diary. Help them write down all their assignments and due dates, and then plan a homework schedule accordingly.

3. **Study together:** Make it a habit to sit with your child while they are studying. Even if you're busy with your own tasks, your mere presence can offer support and minimize distractions.

9.5. Dietary Considerations

Diet can play a role in managing ADHD symptoms. It's important to provide wholesome, nutritionally balanced meals that can help keep your child calm and focused.

1. **Balanced meals:** Make sure your child's diet includes a balance of fruits, vegetables, lean proteins, and whole grains. Avoiding

heavily processed food, sugars, and caffeine can help prevent blood sugar swings, which may aggravate ADHD symptoms.

2. **Proper Hydration:** Staying hydrated is crucial for every individual, but it becomes even more critical when managing ADHD. Dehydration can often manifest as irritability or lack of focus.

Creating an ADHD-friendly home doesn't have to be a daunting task. Remember, the goal is not perfection, but encompassing habits that encourage a structured, loving, and supportive environment. Applying these strategies will give your child the necessary scaffold to manage their symptoms effectively, leading to a happier, healthier home. Don't get disheartened if you encounter challenges. Stay patient, keep learning, and you'll figure out strategies that work best for your family.

As we conclude our journey through 'Practical Strategies: Creating an ADHD-friendly Home and Routine', remember that every family is unique, and what works for one may not work for another. The key is to keep trying, experimenting, learning, and adapting. You're not alone in this. There are resources, communities, and professionals ready to help and guide you. Take heart, for every effort you make is a step towards a brighter, rewarding future for your child.

Chapter 10. Communication is Key: Connecting with Children with ADHD

Establishing a positive and effective communication line with your child, who has ADHD (Attention Deficit Hyperactivity Disorder), illuminates the path to better understanding and facilitates connections that nurture emotional stability and growth. This journey may be fraught with challenges, but being armed with the right knowledge and strategies will aid you in your quest to strengthen your bond with your child.

10.1. Understanding ADHD

ADHD is a neurodevelopmental disorder that manifests in difficulty concentrating, impulsivity, and hyperactivity - symptoms that can considerably impair a child's daily functioning. Contrary to the belief that children with ADHD merely need to "try harder," their symptoms are neurologically rooted, making simple tasks like paying attention or good behavior a daily struggle.

As such, it's essential to recognize the difference between disobedient behavior and ADHD symptoms. This understanding will allow you to better manage your child's behavior, with less infuriation and more empathy.

10.2. Communication: The Path to Understanding

Effective communication is crucial when dealing with ADHD. It builds bridges where gaps existed, fostering a better understanding of the child's world. The first step is being a good listener; it's more about understanding than immediately diving into problem-solving mode. Absorb what the child is saying with patience and openness.

When your child is sharing their feelings, resist the urge to interrupt or downplay their emotions. Validate their feelings and assure them that you are there to provide support. This simple act of listening can strengthen your relationship and make your child feel loved and understood.

10.3. Keeping it Simple and Structured

Children with ADHD can become easily overwhelmed. Consequently, instructions need to be distinct, straightforward, and bear a sense of structure. A simple system can drastically improve communication. Here's an outline:

1. Get your child's full attention: Ensure your child isn't multitasking when you start a conversation.

2. Keep sentences short and interactive: Explain one thing at a time.

3. Use clear and specific language: Avoid abstract terms.

4. Include reminders: Repeat essential points or instructions.

5. Employ visuals: Charts and visual aids can reinforce verbal instructions.

Remember, the aim is to make communication a safe haven for your child, a place with consistency, predictability, and support.

10.4. Building Emotional Intelligence

A child with ADHD often has difficulty recognizing and interpreting emotions, both their own and others'. This impacts social interactions and self-regulation. As a parent, you can help your child build emotional intelligence by:

- Encouraging conversation about feelings: Regularly discuss feelings and emotional reactions.

- Modeling emotional regulation: Show them how to manage and express emotions effectively.

- Reinforcing positive behavior: Compliment your child when they handle their emotions well. Positive reinforcement is a powerful tool.

The progression will be gradual. Celebrate small victories, and don't get disheartened by inevitable setbacks.

10.5. Adjusting Communication Style

Fine-tuning your communication style is essential. It's not just about what you say, but how you say it. Use a calm, firm, and positive tone. Refrain from raising your voice whenever possible; yelling can increase anxiety and does not foster good communication.

Consider using non-verbal forms of communication, like a gentle pat on the shoulder or a warm smile. These gestures can convey your affection and reassurance as effectively as spoken words.

Empower your child by involving them in decision-making processes. Ask for their input on relevant issues, which not only values their opinions but also teaches them critical thinking and problem-solving skills.

10.6. Strategies to Encourage Cooperation

Some days it might seem like getting your child to cooperate is an uphill battle, but applying the following strategies can be beneficial:

- Reward system: Introducing a reward system can help motivate your child to complete tasks and behave appropriately. The rewards can be small, such as additional playtime or a special treat.

- Timers: Using timers can improve time awareness and help your child transition between tasks smoothly.

- Consistency: Children with ADHD respond well to routines, so establish a consistent daily schedule.

Remember, change doesn't happen overnight. Patience, persistence, and plenty of positive reaffirmations are key.

10.7. Embracing ADHD's Positive Traits

While ADHD poses numerous challenges, it is also associated with several positive traits, including creativity, energy, and the ability to think outside the box. By nurturing these abilities and focusing on strengths instead of weaknesses, you not only boost your child's self-esteem but also help them channelize their energies positively.

Sailing the complex waters of parenting or caregiving can be a daunting journey. The process calls for great understanding, patience, and adaptability. However, with the right communication strategies and emotional tools, you can foster a loving, supportive environment that reinforces the connectivity and responsibility needed for children with ADHD to thrive.

Chapter 11. Coping and Thriving: A Toolkit for Parents and Caregivers of Kids with ADHD

ADHD, short for Attention Deficit Hyperactivity Disorder, is a neurodevelopmental condition affecting approximately 5 percent to 10 percent of children worldwide. As a parent or caregiver, it's necessary to have the right tools for navigating the complex maze of emotions, behaviors, and challenges that can occur with your child diagnosed with ADHD. This includes cultivating the ability to nurture their unique strengths, focusing on cultivating positive habits, and implementing well-resourced coping strategies.

11.1. Understanding ADHD: A Brief Overview

Before diving into the world of ADHD specific parenting, it's essential to understand the basics. ADHD is not a reflection of bad parenting, but a neurodevelopmental condition. The hallmark symptoms include difficulty with focus and attention, impulsivity, and hyperactivity, which can result in challenges in academic, social, and family situations. As a parent, these symptoms might feel exhausting and sometimes overwhelming, but remember, with the right strategies and understanding, you can guide your child towards healthier and happier outcomes.

11.2. Recognizing The Positives

Despite the challenges, children with ADHD often have many

strengths - creativity, energy, enthusiasm, an ability to think outside the box, and often a unique perspective on the world around them. Recognizing and encouraging these strengths can provide a confidence boost for your child, fostering self-esteem, resilience, and a positive self-image.

11.3. Building a Structure that Works

Children with ADHD often thrive with routine and structure. A consistent routine provides a sense of security, clarifying expectations and reducing anxiety. Each routine should be customized to suit your child's specific needs. This might involve visual reminders, timers to encourage task completion, and schedule charts.

11.4. Tips for Developing Coping Skills

Developing coping skills is essential for children with ADHD navigating their everyday lives - strategies that provide them tools to manage their symptoms more effectively. This may include tools like:

Skill Builders like: - 'Stop, think, act' practice to curb impulsivity - Breathing exercises for calming - Using planners and organizers for task management

Behavioral Therapies: Behavior Therapy can provide a structured approach for managing ADHD. It helps children control their behavior, understand consequences, and promote positive behavior.

Healthy Lifestyle Habits: Encourage and model healthy lifestyle habits, including regular exercise, a balanced diet, and sufficient sleep.

Role-Playing Scenarios: Role-playing can help children learn and practice new skills while also providing an opportunity to apply these skills in a controlled environment.

11.5. Engaging With Your Child's School

Working collaboratively with your child's school is crucial. By keeping open lines of communication, you can ensure that necessary adjustments are made for your child's learning and behavioral needs.

11.6. Forming a Support Network

Build a support network for you and your child. It could be friends, fellow parents, ADHD support groups, or professional therapists. You are not alone on this journey. Recognize your emotional needs and reach out for support when you need it.

Keep in mind, your child's journey with ADHD is not merely about managing symptoms; it's about thriving within them, learning to harness their unique abilities, and working towards their fullest potential. It's about resilience, growth, and most importantly, unending love. As their parent or caregiver, you are the most valuable asset they have in this journey. Armed with the right tools and understanding, you are undeniably on the path to turning ADHD related meltdowns into moments of growth, understanding, and connection.